Awake from Ego

Creation within the 2 Basic Languages of Human Beings

Awake from Ego

Creation within the 2 Basic Languages of Human Beings

Joe Zubrzycki

Marco Island, FL * Lionheart Consultants

Copyright © 2018 by Joe Zubrzycki

Cover Art by Dr. Steve Hinkey

Cover Design by Cierra Cole Consulting

Book Content Design by Building Bridges Consulting

All rights reserved. This book or any portion thereof may not be reproduced or used in any manner whatsoever without the express written permission of the publisher except for the use of brief quotations in a book review.

Printed in the United States of America

First Printing, 2018

ISBN-10: 1-948640-00-7

ISBN-13: 978-1-948640-00-8

Lionheart Consultants

Marco Island, FL

www.awakefromego.com

Dedication

From our loving tribe of ancient ancestors to our current family and friends___

The intention for us to remember we are human beings regardless of our doings ___

To those of you who are seeking may you find your stillness rest or launch station___

For those who are in despair may you open your door to allow your creation you hold the key___

May you look within to see eternal love to see the truth that is you___

May you awake with joyous freedom understanding every day is a gift___

May you share your unique art gifts insights for our human evolution___

Contents

Dedication v

Foreword ix

Preface xiii

Acknowledgments xv

Section One 1

    1 – Time and the 2 Basic Human Languages___ 3

    2 – Shining a Light on Ego Fear___ 5

    3 – Ego Structure___ 7

    4 – The Evolution of the Human Mind___ 9

    5 – Awareness of Eternal Time___ 11

    6 – The Two Basic Human Languages of Earth___ 13

    7 – Awareness to Our Emotional State___ 14

    8 – Remembered Awareness Gifts Seen___ 17

    9 – Unlimited Possibilities Start from Within___ 19

Section Two 21

    Introduction___ 23

    Invitation___ 25

    Freedom of Formation___ 27

    Our Next Meeting with Awareness___ 29

    Gratitude Manifesting Abundance___ 31

    Now We Thrive___ 33

    Worlds Our Word Creates___ 35

    Smile of Gratitude___ 37

    Being with All___ 39

    Old Energy to New___ 41

    Meditation to Creation___ 43

    Empathy Doorway Understanding___ 45

    Healing Unity Harmony___ 47

    All That We Need___ 49

    From Special to Sacred Relationship___ 51

Show Up	53
Power of One	55
Personal Freedom	57
Ours to Carry	59
Release the Luggage	61
Dynamic Collective	63
Awakened Walk	65
Path of Adjustments	67
Momentum of Being	69
Catharsis Crucible Freedom	71
Helpful Gratitude Purpose	73
Alone Lost to Awakened	75
Group Gathering Purpose	77
Intuitive Servant Heart	79
We are the Bridge	81
Stillness Held	83
I Appreciate You	85
Free Flowing	87
Remembrance Beauty Abundance	89
Vulnerability to Courage	91
Storm Rolling In	93
Conclusion	95
About the Author	97
About the Cover Artist	98

Foreword

"<u>Awake from Ego</u> is my journey of meditation to creation shared with you___"

I've had the privilege of being an honored guest in Joe's life over the past few years as his executive coach. Seeing his meditative journey unfold through our coaching partnership and his commitment to grow continues to produce awe and gratitude within me. My mind and heart can remember in an instant the moment of our first session. Before me was a man with a firm commitment to gift the world with a guide to experience freedom, ease and play.

It was evident that Joe was a dedicated student seeking truth. With every resource he referenced, there was an accompanied note of how he had read it as many times as needed to have it soak into his core. At our second meeting, I heard of how intentional he was in preparing to write his first excerpt for <u>Awake from Ego</u>. His initial recipe for creating this work involved meditation and tai chi while setting aside time for play with an inspiring documentary or hilarious comedy. His ability to dance from focus to play was delightful and awakened me to how I could benefit from infusing more play into my work.

By our third meeting, I observed two things. The first was that Joe had, with ease and play, created several pieces for <u>Awake from Ego</u>. In witnessing this, I imagined that his intention to write <u>Awake from Ego</u> that year would be complete within three months. The second thing that I observed was something all too common of the leaders I work with who have a drive and commitment to contribute greatly to humanity. What I saw and heard in his tone was frustration. Frustration mainly with others. For clients who invest heavily, both in time and energy, in living great lives and leaving the world better than they found it, there is a tendency to experience irritation when they observe others repeatedly making things difficult for those around them. This frustration is often compounded by the pressure they place on themselves to produce excellent results, on-time, consistently. Like the chicken and egg situation, wondering which came first, it's difficult to distinguish what is at the core of their frustration – them self or others?

By the second month of our engagement, Joe discovered a missing piece in his creative work. This missing piece was the experience of freedom. Month by month for the next few years, Joe would look at important areas of his life where he saw possibilities for greater freedom. With love, commitment and compassion he strengthened relationships and released limiting beliefs. With each opportunity to grow, he chose love and realized how his ego would gain attention and lure him away from truth. He discovered his own symbolic version of bringing a sword and shield to conversations and how to release this conditioned pattern of a need for protection. In doing so, he could more compassionately notice another's version of protection and respond with love.

In this book, Joe Zubrzycki describes an alternative path for your life; releasing fear, ego, darkness, overwhelm and disconnection.

He achieves this in an easy-to-read structure that can both be understood in an instant, as well as be pondered for a lifetime. This book is an excellent gift to give oneself whether read in a weekend or kept by your side to open at any page amidst your days, even the fullest of them.

As a certified and experienced executive coach who guides others in experiencing heaven on earth more fully, this gift that Joe has created brings me a sense of peace and strength for the future. He has done the work to show us a path where we can embrace our ego and humanity while nourishing our relationship with our soul/spirit. This is a resource that meets you where you are and provides partnership for the challenges you face and the dreams that yearn to be birthed within you.

"The whole of creation is veiled to us we are here on earth away from spirit home___"

Life at times can feel challenging. There is no manual. What works for some, may not be best for you. <u>Awake from Ego</u> provides a framework to experience greater love and light in your world.

At a time when the world appears to be fear filled, Joe reminds us that this is an illusion – freedom, ease and play are available.

"With more concentrated light through pausing embracing ease we see awareness truth___"

Will you give yourself permission to pause, if only for a moment, to imagine your life with more love and light?

This man's commitment to himself, his family and the world brings me to tears of joy. This work has been cultivated over several years. Each time Joe would sit down to write, there was an unwavering commitment to come from love and to do the groundwork of centering himself and rooting in love before sitting down to share this wisdom with you. Thank you, Joe.

Melanie Perry, MA, PCC

Executive Coach and Consultant

Perry Coaching & Consulting LLC

Preface

Awake from Ego is my journey of meditation to creation shared with you___

The intention is to encourage a journey of meditative being into the flow of your art or creation___

Words are things as they manifest into our world___

We as humans only think and speak in two basic languages - eternal love or ego fear___

Time's only truth is in the now… past and future are simply fragmented illusions___

Being in the now awareness is a comfort for our ego when wrapped within soul and spirit___

Within the ease of your meditation your art your creation will flow in the symphony of colors___

Be aware of the emotions we are playing out into our world___

Be mindful to pause when the ego fear is imprisoning us___

Eternal love is our freedom in creation manifesting abundance___

Acknowledgments

Niquenya D. Collins, Master Business Coach, President & CEO Building Bridges Consulting

Niquenya, thank you for your coaching expertise, spiritual and business intuition along with a precise, direct approach to launch this work within 3 months. Most importantly, thank you for your encouragement to stay within the style and expression that comes through the spiritual meditation experience.

Melanie Perry, MA, PCC Executive Coach and Consultant Perry Coaching

I am joyously grateful in our coaching journey for my continuing transformation into a progression of freedom, ease and artistic creation in all facets of life. Thank you for capturing this heartfelt remembrance for all of us in the foreword of this book.

Martha Linn, D.C. In Radiant Health

All love and appreciation for your healing, intuitive energy through love compassion joy. Much gratitude for your introduction to Dr. Steve Hinkey, and our progressions with group meditation healing and inclusive spirit of all. You have been the calming healer guiding this paradigm shift from an old world of stagnation into the world of innovations and visionary creation of today.

Dr. Steve Hinkey

Artist, healer and dear friend, you have always inspired me to search for more regarding our evolution of the mind as human beings. Steve your healing art is transformational energy at joyous play. Thank you for your dynamic creation of the front and back cover art for this book.

Dearly departed father Eugene was a deep thinker of simple truths and observations of life and business. Two of his more memorable sayings were "It's a sin to worry because in that moment you are thinking without faith" and "My Holy Spirit tells me." Even though our relationship was difficult and highly conflicted… many gems of awareness are born from this experience.

Mother Angela has always been a beacon of pure joy laughter and acceptance. A teacher of harmony within home and workplace. Her great intention has always been to choose laughter over tears.

Dearly departed brother Eugene was a protector with an inquisitive mind and a lover of innovative technologies. His courage and endearing humor was our bridge into the U.S., our new world.

Sister Angie full of strength in all adversities while holding peace joy calming poise and sharing love with all. Dear older sister teacher and at times parent thank you for your patience.

Sister Bernice manifesting thoughts and words into art creation beauty of your life within family and business. Thank you for the many years of dramatic and humorous adventures growing up and with our partnership in business.

Dearest wife Michelle full of peace sharing our love our family and our partnership in this evolving life together. Michelle my love, thank you for your grace within our abundant life journey. Your quick humor and joyous ease holds us all within peaceful harmony.

Beloved son Jacob born and evolved into an abstract mind and sharp hilarious wit. Much love and appreciation for your powerful independence and quest for freedom. I enjoy our joyful cosmic game of catch within our exchange of abstract thoughts and concepts.

Beloved son Steven born and evolved into leadership by example and generous engaging wit. Much love and appreciation for your giving nature and peaceful calm. I enjoy our many conversations about life and career as well as our love for baseball.

Spiritual brother and friend Paul Schmidt thank you for our journey from high school to the current time. You graciously welcomed me into your family through those turbulent teenage years which was truly a Godsend. Thank you for your humor and thought-provoking life and spiritual conversations.

Spiritual brother and friend Steve Clements thank you for sharing your spiritual walk. Through your love of God, you have filled our meetings and conversations with wisdom grace and joyful encouragement.

Spiritual brother and friend Chris Metz thank you for your generosity and kindness through a transitional time in our life. Your introduction to <u>A Course in Miracles</u> and continued encouragement to study this work has proven to be a pivotal inspiration for my art creation work and play.

Spiritual brother and friend Mark Davids thank you for sharing in your quest for more understanding of all spiritual things and beings from past and today. It's always a pure joy to connect and compare our newest awareness and the progressions moving forward.

Spiritual brother and friend Bill Ganz thank you for your inspired intentional unlimited daily walk. You encourage everyone around you to strive for the fullest in life. Your vision and kindness for all humanity is clearly evident in the genius of your diverse talents and gifts.

Thank you to all the wonderful beings that have shared their lives with my life ___
Whether our time shared was for a few impactful moments or a lifetime of friendship___
Thank you and may you all be in joyous ease creation… until we meet again___

Section One

1 – Time and the 2 Basic Human Languages___

We speak and therefore think in only two basic languages___

As human beings on earth the two languages spoken are ego fear or eternal love___

Our quest for freedom search for truth and breakthrough to understand___

And again we step into our daily walk of release___

The release of thoughts and things that no longer serve us___

The release from ego choices to serve false gods... social acceptance security earthly love___

The release of ego illusion found in physical body intellect excluding spirit soul intuitive___

Our human evolution of the mind is to embrace ego with our soul and spirit engaged___

In the lost illusion of fear ego reactionary attacks upon others is in turn an attack on ourselves___

Accept and take the key of eternal love for the release of our self-imprisoned illusion___

Open to fullest sight in eternal love___

Open to knowing the truth is... Divine eternal will___

Shining light onto ego illusion structure of free will___

Awareness the step into duality uncovered___

Our old choice was from past driven ego fear lost illusion into self-imprisoned false freedom___

Our awareness choice of eternal love allowing sharing creating living joy___

2 – Shining a Light on Ego Fear___

Ego structure... Ego imprisonment... Uncovering the ego illusion___

Our structure of human existence on earth is of three parts___

We as humans on earth are ego/body and soul and spirit___

Pure ego is survival in the physical material realm alone separate from all___

Alone our ego is without awareness of all___

The whole of creation is veiled to us we are here on earth away from spirit home___

In time we find the illusion of past and future___

Welcome to the now the only truth in time___

Lost in past or future is the state of too busy... Exhaustion disease being without ease___

Lost in never having enough time is the illusion... Lost in self and fragmented away from all___

Time in the now is to enjoy the present___

The gift of joy accepted in the sacred now___

The illusion of happiness is chased between past and future time___

All the while avoiding the only reality... The now___

So in our daily step remember to pause in the truth of joy the truth of now___

Carry the awakened meditative morning into our awareness throughout our day___

3 – Ego Structure___

When in pure ego the soul and the spirit has been forgotten___

In the forgotten state of pure ego we are at the worst of our humanity___

If we remain lost in fear survival we will lose the truth of humanity for the future___

Ego fear in our past was perceived as needed without the remembrance of soul and spirit___

Ego fear is fragmented understanding based on illusionary foundation leading to false structure___

The ego structure seems very complex at first awareness___

The illusion of ego structure is seen in the worst of our human history___

With more concentrated light through pausing embracing ease we see awareness truth___

Ego structure is based in the false concept of lack scarcity___

With the lighted path of awareness we see abundance in every step of our day___

This illusion of lack and scarcity has been beset in every aspect of our lives through ego___

False facts were created to justify such false beliefs as human slavery___

Can we awaken as humans to see the insanity of these many false beliefs___

What ego structured false beliefs are we enslaved in today___

Slavery exists today in so many forms through complex structures of pure ego___

Our human evolution of mind is the light we shine upon our own individual release from slavery___

With each human mind awakened the organic nature of creation will flourish thrive in all of us___

Now is the time for human Evolution of the mind___

A second of awareness is the expansive momentum into our eternity into eternal love___

In the now allow the light into our individual ego embraced with soul and spirit___

Freedom from the ways of despair and isolation of pure ego___

Our salvation our redemption is to give this awareness light to each other___

Our being is to share the eternal love when we first allow it for ourselves to be within us___

Shared eternal love with all our brothers and sisters without judgment___

When we judge others while lost in fear we also judge ourselves in pure ego___

Atonement is the spirit release of our ego selfishness in past action___

Atonement is Forgiveness allowed by the spirit... our spirit for our release for each other___

In true wholeness of soul spirit and ego we find our freedom we find our evolution___

4 – The Evolution of the Human Mind___

Our daily step into constant awareness of contrast___

Pure light or pure darkness is without seeing___

The choice: to be the light in the darkness___

To be the guide to allow others to love us___

To show love compassion to be still to awaken___

To awaken from ego into the light of eternal love___

The goal to assist in the evolution of the human mind___

In this work/play human mind evolution throughout all time evolving in the now___

Our current walk takes us to the illusion of betrayal and social acceptance___

Ego fuels fear hatred violence into this world by reactionary thoughts and actions___

Pure ego fragmented disconnected from the whole of being with soul and spirit___

Pure ego destructive fire unrecognizable human actions seek spirit's atonement___

Emotions recognized remembrance delivered our awakening in time our saving grace___

In awakening from illusion of past hurt to understanding past time is only a sliver of reality___

In awakening to the meditative awareness breath we see through the veiled darkness ego fear___

In meditative awakening through time and space into intuitive remembrance our humanity truth___

5 – Awareness of Eternal Time___

Spirit Thought Translation___

Eternal love all spiritual unaffected by ego___

Our awakening into this understanding eternal love to be with all___

Our awakening for all beings are our saving faith as we are one with eternal love___

One with individual freedom connected light___

Freedom to create to assist to innovate to evolve___

To evolve in meditative intuitive allowing eternal love translation of heaven onto earth___

Spirit thought translation for growth for more ease for simple joy___

Our joyous gift being in eternal love belonging in freedom creation throughout time___

Understanding contrast with our faith our light within the giving and allowing to all___

Time the Truth of the Now___

The now awakened in the sacred second intuition meditative spirit guide___

Understanding the place for past and the dreams of future___

In the ease of freedom from soul lives lived in emotional imprisoned burden___

Reactionary past actions now understood healed and released by atonement of spirit___

In freedom past understood as sliver of whole in illusion fragmentation___

Wholeness to be to connect to see to remember truth eternal love___

A sliver of time passed in judgment misguided fear ego___

Atonement spirit guide healing into truth creation___

So today we step and release evolutionary past for the false fear it was___

Forgiveness of self then forgiveness for each other then atonement through spirit guide___

Free from judgment betrayals social tyranny false belonging___

Freedom into eternal love truth joy belonging within abundance___

Our Release in the Now of Time___

Allowing light eternal love for the ego perception of time into awakened transformation___

Flexible structure of light into ego into awakening___

In the stillness meditation only one truth eternal love___

All creation all pure love into the all of being___

Evolutionary process of the human mind awareness meditative action in the now___

We do not need to evolve when we are in the spirit world___

We need our spirit guide in our evolution of human mind for this translation on earth___

When we are in the sliver of time blinded by judgment our path back is in stillness meditative___

Stillness into ease into meditation into sight and to calming ease awareness freedom___

With illusion fear ego we have built the fragmented present state of our world___

See now from above with spirit all others all in ease joyous peace___

See now freedom from betrayal illusion fear ego___

See now freedom from judgment imprisonment of isolation___

See now freedom from despair social acceptance ego fear punishment___

Our release from the violent triggered emotions of past lost in fear___

Our release in the joyous ease of life lived in the now with eternal love___

6 – The Two Basic Human Languages of Earth___

The two basic languages we as humans speak are eternal love or ego fear___

Awareness of the emotions we feel think speak and act leads to the recognition___

Awareness of the language we build our world our life with for each other___

Eternal love is the language of abundance creation___

Eternal love is spirit soul and ego enlightened in wholeness___

Fear ego is the language of illusion structure with self-hatred survival in past false facts___

Of the two languages fear ego is currently programmed into our actions___

Fear ego is for illusionary survival of the past for the imprisonment of human beings___

Awareness of this ego fear illusion is our evolution into eternal love___

Eternal love thoughts words actions create manifest human mind evolution___

Remembrance of our spiritual being in the now joyous freedom___

Freedom from the hatred-built ego fear structures of past imprisonments___

Awareness stillness meditation intention the light to truly see___

In the now we look at ego fear as it truly is lost and misguided___

Ego freedom of fear illusion is transformed with the embrace of soul and spirit___

In the now we remember the awareness of two languages___

In the now we declare our freedom by shining the light on illusion fear___

In the eternal love the eternal now we allow ourselves to think speak create a joyous world___

Create now our artist human mind free from illusion fear ego___

Create now our awareness with each other by being eternal love___

7 – Awareness to Our Emotional State___

Only two true languages are spoken in human life on earth___

Our words thoughts and actions are manifesting the world around us___

Awareness to the language software we allow to run our brain as the hardware___

Please add the words that come to you naturally throughout the walk of your day___

The space provided is an invitation for your awareness to the language you speak daily___

May the choice of eternal love language light our path to enlightenment evolution___

Eternal love	*Ego fear*
Allowing all	*Isolation/separation*
Whole	*Fragmented*
Seeing awareness	*Blinded reaction*
Compassion	*Judgment/punishment*
Freedom flight unlimited	*Imprisoned trapped in despair*
Sight	*Darkness*
Peaceful	*Troubled*

8 – Remembered Awareness Gifts Seen___

Remembrance our gift to see feel gratitude into the new day___

Faith our willingness to listen to our intuitive... all is a gift___

Our intuitive our constant our connection our spirit___

Renewed guided by eternal love into peaceful ease daily___

Our way through spirit to heart relationship to the awareness divine___

Our step with the spiritual allowing ourselves to share and give freely___

Our only true earthly relationship is with our spirit___

And spirit awareness guidance given to atone soul and ego___

Atonement is the work/play of our spirit___

Freedom of fear ego control and judgment... freedom from self-imprisonment___

False ego memories appearing real released by our spirit through atonement___

Truth divine awareness harmony ours always found in the allowing of being in the now___

Veiled is our truth divine sight until again we allow the ease of being with our spirit___

Our breath our compassion our brothers and sisters imprisoned release our salvation___

Our only doing is to be in the now eternal love for each other___

9 – Unlimited Possibilities Start from Within___

And so we come to the step we take daily___

And in the daily commitment to awareness we work/play with our spirit___

Awareness momentum being in the now we all assist in the evolution of our human mind___

Meditative stillness allowed by our intention to create to manifest to allow eternal love___

Search our mind search our emotions true healing of ego and soul through spirit mind map___

As unlimited as stars in the multiverse we are uniquely needed to be the symphony of creation___

Our way into intention prayer meditation stillness allowing gratitude beauty ease___

Our way into meditation through the work/play of mind mapping our heart feeling for direction___

Using the language thoughts and actions of eternal love shape our day to live in is creation___

And so we step into our day with the intentionality of being sharing evolving as human beings___

Welcome to allowing the flow of eternal love into meditation mind mapping___

Please remember to bring play into your day have fun with meditation mind mapping___

Welcome to my version of a meditation mind map____
Please remember to bring play into your day have fun____

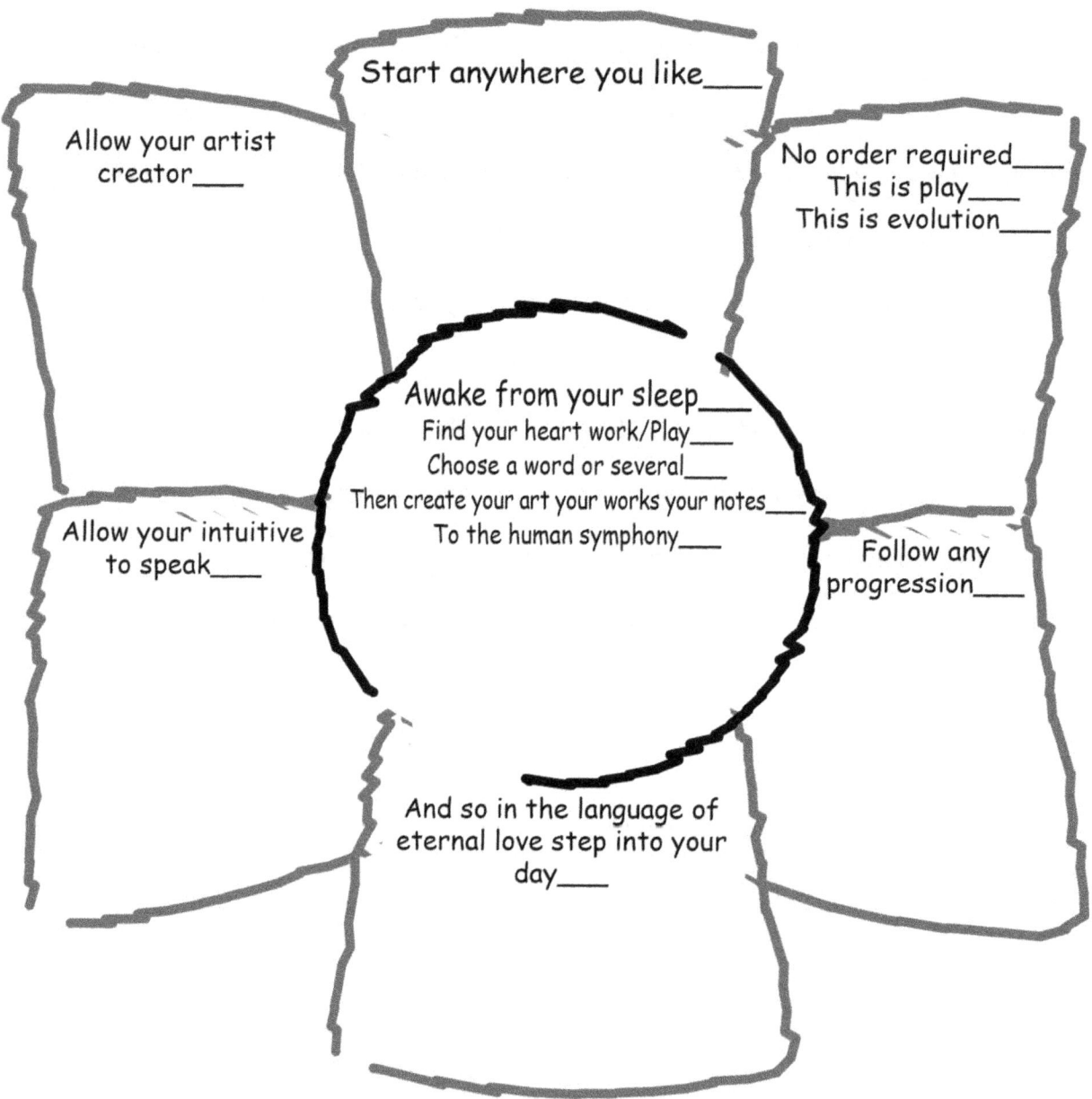

Start anywhere you like____

Allow your artist creator____

No order required____
This is play____
This is evolution____

Awake from your sleep____
Find your heart work/Play____
Choose a word or several____
Then create your art your works your notes____
To the human symphony____

Allow your intuitive to speak____

Follow any progression____

And so in the language of eternal love step into your day____

Section Two

Introduction___

Welcome to section 2 of this work/play... awake from ego___

Sharing my work/play with you is a true joy and hope/dream to release your artist your truth___

Thank you... heartfelt gratitude appreciation and anticipation to see your work/play___

May you be kind and full of love and courage for yourself___

The use of the language of eternal love starts from within yourself___

Dear brothers and sisters find your rest or insight or launch throughout this art creation___

My hope is for you to find the eternal love words that speak to your daily step___

Invitation___

We are on the journey of our selves___

An awareness of how we engage with life___

There is no manual for this adventurous game___

So we form our own rules boundaries and beliefs___

At a certain point we transcend into more___

When we decide the choices are up to us from within___

This is the leadership ownership declaration of our life___

The statement that is our own spirit message___

Unlimited possibilities start from within___

This is my awareness spirit message___

Soon you may want to share your awareness art with us___

It's a symphony of art with all our distinctive individuality___

The sounds align in the beauty of us all in creation___

Freedom of Formation___

Freedom of Formation___

Whatever it is___

It must be a progression___

A living art___

Title it – name it – box it in and that is all it will ever be... limited___

Like a changing river makes a new way___

See the way in the intuitive knowing of now___

The opportunities present and show themselves___

Be there in the stillness of a second in time to see___

Be the freedom to see in the now___

Our Next Meeting with Awareness___

How did we arrive at our last meeting___

Was it with a shield or a sword for protection___

If a weapon is held in defense it is already manifesting an attack in our mind___

Now imagine arriving without a weapon... without ego___

Own how that would feel... being your true essence of creation___

Look to coach to learn to play in the true process of sharing___

In this ease of exchange of thoughts visions and dreams is our playground of creation___

In this freedom of sharing expression we bring out our best in each other___

In this awareness of co-creation we manifest an ease of completion an ego free agenda___

Gratitude Manifesting Abundance___

What if we awake to gratitude to truth___

In the first remembrance of our day___

Yes the tasks will be done___

In creation our allowing our knowing our being___

What if we see the ease inside of our everyday tasks___

Awakening to the knowing that our only purpose is to be___

A bridge for another living being___

So our base truth is to truly see the ones we connect with___

In that we naturally bring our gifts___

The gifts that are always with us___

The gifts that are us___

And we share our gifts overflowing___

In the compounding eternal replenishment to the more we give we receive as well___

So everyone receives… what they think they need___

Until we all see ease gratitude manifesting abundance___

Awake from ego and the illusion of need want and lack___

To the remembrance of the joyous beings we are in eternal love___

Now We Thrive___

Today the world___

All around us in our awakening___

Past and future joust in clouded field___

Centered stillness is the seed of now___

Enter knowing joy as gift freely ours___

Enter knowing outside of eternal love we see only fear___

Worlds Our Word Creates___

In our awareness is seen the words chosen manifested___

As real as bricks or atoms to become what surrounds us___

Stillness first is the sunrise to our chosen day___

Meditation tranquillity spirit soul infused ego___

So we see our words are the compass that paints our reality___

With brush wave of stillness inclusion comfort ease we are in the now___

And our inner spirit guide whispers the now the music the background divine___

Simple truth ego when with spirit and soul can hear this world's intuitive language___

Take intention to seek the way by every word's chosen creation___

Take intention every breath be for unified self then into unified world___

Smile of Gratitude___

Smile of gratitude as easy as sunrise cascades nurturing___

Appreciation table set full welcoming warmth fellowship___

Solutions sprout calm effortless mind intuitive___

Most powerful energy abundance in present sun's ray___

Ease of the little we give to total harvest full sunset___

Compounding addition seeds growth by ease of eternal love___

Already done already given simply awaiting our remembrance___

Gratitude lights our way down chosen days path___

More than enough given effortless by divine sun's ray___

More than enough for us to extend gratitude smile eternal love___

Being with All___

How we treat ourselves is how we treat the world___

Our relationship with all source divine are the eyes we see with___

Our vision is what and how we see ourselves in everyone___

When our friend is lost our light is needed to be a beacon of the way___

The light we have is so easy to give and in co-creation is our joyful purpose to share___

Witness the breath of eternal love as all that is needed a simple smile for joyous friend___

The daily steps we take with everyday words we build our world awakened___

Awakened by that love not material a love translated from spirit to be this world___

The world seemingly in far off horizon is in truth eternal love already with us being in the now___

Light awareness vision and dear smile gratitude is eternal love being with all___

Old Energy to New___

Growth organic as rain to sun to soil to green___

As old energy to new transforming flow of disruption to cooperation___

As rocks stand in rivers flow we are transformed to smooth gems by our experiences___

Progression translation evolution being always as change as growth___

The grand illusion carved in sliver of time remembered rigid past___

Our release being in stillness in awareness healing sight awakened freedom ___

Storms arrive as egos collide in meetings over abundant opportunity___

Calm effort slows emotional storm to sight to pathway to empathy understanding___

Meditation to Creation___

Our quiet space sacred time reflection in the now___

Our spirit intuitive thoughts flow patterns systems of all creation___

Light infused soul spirit to ego begins creative wholeness of mind___

Wholeness with the inclusion stillness centeredness acceptance of gratitude___

Freedom from murky water separation desperation illusions ego fear___

Formed contrast seen coming together with thriving abundance momentum___

We can bring the all of creation with meditative sight to be in the now___

We can receive effortless source eternal love in the giving of this to each other___

Empathy Doorway Understanding___

Understanding courageous search experience subtle waves caress___

Perseverance faith fed spring endless cascading bounty our nourishment___

Path laid trusting contrasting reflections strength and grace to banish false fear___

Judgement laid down empathy glance transcends us to soulful ease in being___

Every step as first breath exhilaration seeking knowing early morning light___

Every power drawn upon purposeful entry through doorway empathy sight___

Healing Unity Harmony___

Healing allowing accepting uniqueness fully played joyous life___

Integrated song dance art ego spirit soul___

Triangulation replenishing energy universal intuitive pattern___

Compounding addition Fibonacci way divine innovated balance___

Tide waves breath taken ground air water space eternal creation___

From limited to the harmony always divine intuitive___

From fear to the forever healing unity eternal love___

All That We Need___

Many times what we need shows up as distasteful unwanted pure ego___

Pure ego animal reaction survival remembrance hurt awakens anger hate ___

Again as oceans wave comes unrelenting awaiting our release of illusion fear___

Illusion ego fear accepted will produce ceremonial reliving of loss bitterness darkness___

So we sleep at days end to awaken once again with sunrise symbol eternal love___

And again we step forward in our day to share brilliance simple smile gratitude___

In return we receive what we give by intent intuitive heart___

Salvation by giving soul spirit eternal love our only way to peace___

From Special to Sacred Relationship___

Is our hope chained to physical reward to final denial truth eternal___

Are we alone separate awaiting translation sight ego soul spirit wholeness___

Take a picture precious capture sacred second proof of time seen___

From special relationship emotion to translation unity of the wholeness of being___

Our sacred relationship is of evolution ego soul spirit as one in human form___

Achievement in old world old human rules broken forever – time for release of all time___

In the release of time past and future to the only eternal now___

The sacred way of spirit soul with ego embraced is our understanding humanity evolved___

Recognition remembrance giving birth evolution to our higher self-serving our humanity___

We are – our freedom is in recognition wholeness ego soul spirit in human form___

Show Up___

Unforeseen unthinkable disruptive shifts in expectations___

Engaged in the process to bring our needed sacred purpose___

Courage in vulnerability willful sharing our soul essence___

Show up – Be present to the gifts the universal divine is manifesting___

Unforeseen journey challenged tried agitated disregarded___

Engage that gem the formation of our evolving self being more than enough___

Courage our friend our voice to offer to be still to allow to share___

Show up – Be present to the gifts the universal divine is manifesting___

Power of One___

Commitment exploration understanding search for wholeness___

The one that is three parts combined in this physical human realm___

Allness wholeness connectedness joyousness manifested___

Courage vulnerability shift from fear to eternal love kindest touch___

Desperation illusion separateness left aside for good___

Awareness in the now allows us our work/play of lifting up the sea of human down cast eyes___

All together we are the journey seeking to come together in the now___

I am you and you are me and we are all one in the now___

Personal Freedom___

Freedom requires extreme inner reflection perseverance of storm to calm___

Splash the light on deepest darkest place hidden freedoms key awaiting release___

Protection safety security fear swept away with free will faith eternal love___

Declaration standing in stillness tranquillity ease of soul spirit group life___

Such a simple ask... such a simple awareness___

Holy spirit take away that which is not mine to carry___

Ours to Carry___

Carry what you will in ego projections until time's end___

Judgement jury born ego love of barter trade purchase___

Man's dogma words fear egos captured faithless toil___

Ours to carry is truth light as breath joyous gratitude ease remembered___

Eternal love given freely effortlessly to our everyday ebb and flow___

Release into eternal will… freedom pure process crucible___

Freedom for all of us to be out of times cage into eternal sacred awareness the now___

Universal Fibonacci spiral sequence divine formation ease remembered___

Release the Luggage___

Let it go... Freedom is all in the release of yesterday's clinging ego fear___

Rise up wake up from ego to the gift of ease divine bliss in gratitude___

Our ego wrapped in soul spirit deserves to come along laughing for this new ride___

Sharing with all of soul spirit ego/personality only pathway to conscious wholeness___

Letting go of who where when what went wrong because it's alright now after all___

Judging is the burdensome heavy luggage... let it go ascend to freedom___

Ascend through and beyond it all with ease soul spirit and ego calmed by eternal love___

Awaken to see the true light of our belonging in eternal love ours for all of time___

Dynamic Collective___

In the group talent shared heart compass pointed direction___

Ease energy purpose passion contrast resolution friend___

Bold belonging strength stance empathy path joined___

Laughter's wave gratitude song unrehearsed momentum found freedom___

Joy lasting stillness captured for reflection glance future doorway___

Through the swing of bandwidth into collaborative understanding mission purpose___

Awakened Walk___

Tuned in vibration release love serving others in awareness self___

Vibration unity with individual art translation complete___

Vast inter world group wholeness tapestry ego soul spirit rejoined___

Awakened walk step up into eons of vision cascading symphony past___

Clearing remembered our being masterful presence allowing ease___

Vortex structure motion energy building universal understanding in the now___

Path of Adjustments___

Simple constant adjustments free of past expectations experiences___

To see anew allowing today's formation unprejudiced... free of illusion___

Eternal heart accepting simple new meetings as a chance to help to unveil___

The past swept away with clearing spirit guidance freedom for the asking___

Refreshed from burden free brisk walk illuminated gratitude journeys path of faith___

Breath of joyous ease our song of intuitive ancestral knowing into our heart's path___

Momentum of Being___

In the now a stillness suspended view___

Vortex flow received in being simply connected___

Daily our step in only commitment to help and lift up___

Recharged rejuvenated sustained in breath in living in ease___

Seeing recognition of eon's fullest panoramic vantage tranquillity___

Today anew awaited gifted accepted cherished and given to be shared___

In the motion of the momentum extending love eternal gratitude in simple smile___

Awakened to effortless being in tribal ancestral richness acknowledged shared remembered___

Catharsis Crucible Freedom___

In the growth to personal transformation to sight from shadow to light___

In the allowing of our passage through the eye of the needle to be seen by each other___

Freedom the sound felt shared in laughter's roar joyous awakened recognition___

Purpose we share what is soul pain released by giving our help away in freedom___

With our brothers and sisters we step together to offer to heal to comfort to create___

With meditative energy and universal spirit we are playground artists sharing cheerful courage___

Again we step into our day shared___

Again we step never alone again___

Helpful Gratitude Purpose___

We step into our day full of sacred moments___

We step to greet to help those awaiting release past vibration effect___

Guided by subtle adjustments of eternal love into our eternal will___

Guided by gentle smiles of recognition laughter remembrance___

Ease gracious flow cascading awareness___

Eternal love being with energy universal organic___

Action with nature's being – step into joyous life purpose play___

Ours now as always – ours now more clearly seen___

Awake to kindness old friend ego has brought contrast to see light___

Awake to personality/ego now as dawn awakens us with spirit soul___

Awake to gentleness as inner child receives nourishment___

Awake to realization our wholeness connected comfort of all___

Alone Lost to Awakened___

Alone the feeling so real in the separated state of physical ego fear realm___

Lost in the pain so real the struggle set as a projected expectation projected belief___

Startled by the illusion interruption of ego fear upon truth peaceful being___

Remembrance in a sacred second of awareness that eternal love is true being___

Universal light given the contrast ego fear to unveil truth reality consciousness___

Truth seen in stillness calm and expand extend eternal love our only gift our only need___

Trust in simple daily gratitude stillness of being eternal love___

Trust in powerful calm connected consciousness eternal love___

Group Gathering Purpose___

Strength and weakness ego wrapped in blanket spirit soul___

Our pattern woven of wounded love past tender youth___

Carried hurt manifesting tangible foundation in far off isolation past___

Fortress armed vigilante guard promised defense certain attack___

Ray of light meditation intent touching stones path spoken pure___

Smile to laughter knowing duality's journey sharing voice to found self___

Voice in heart empathy felt and worn by choice in new path only dreamed before___

Vision's calm manifested now in second of thought in awakened mind___

Words building shapes pour through as tears release bitter veiled wound___

For you and me vulnerability breeds strength from fear to embraced eternal love___

Intuitive Servant Heart___

Stillness calm reflection eternal love___

Ease in morning mist daylights ray unveils our release___

Born anew in sunrise whispering warm breath___

Caressing clovers a remembrance of moon light blanket past___

Being in creation knowing ease truth nourishment___

Heart natural attraction flower eternal love___

Align connect once again with longing passion purpose___

Our intuitive servant heart instrument playing universal symphony___

We are the Bridge___

Our words in meditative intention___

Intuitive linguist manifesting playground sky___

Sunflower soul sky rain transformed celestial wine___

Thoughts build within winds surfing through leaves rushing song___

Inside the sacred instant time translation heaven accepted___

World in the now woven life with aspiration of divine continuum___

Animal plant and mineral realms open celebration with ego wrapped spirit soul___

Our gift our words our dreams the bridge realized in conscious awakened ego___

Stillness Held___

Stillness the morning breath awaken to passion purpose step___

Grounded the ease of resting under summer green leafed shade___

Lifted by thousands of tender grass blades into the softness of angels transformed___

Song wind rushing in with leaves breath filtered sun rays dance___

Suspended in this world between worlds to hear to see intuitive knowing___

Being still... being with... being part of being wholeness___

Empathy to understanding of ego self to awakened human being___

Truth eternal love in strongest calm gratitude ease stillness held___

I Appreciate You___

The sound intersecting the horizon of eternal love___

I appreciate you___

Boldly for being all you are___

Kindly for your energy creating your art___

Sharing the uniqueness reflecting we are one and all___

Bring and share again today the priceless diamond you are___

And shine your freedom felt in stillness courage___

The reflection the remembrance we are all one___

I appreciate you... how beautiful that sounds___

I appreciate you... how shared gratitude feels___

How gracious the effect of down cast eyes lifting up and souls awakening___

Free Flowing___

Let's take the river and ride in natural flow___

In the ease – all that ease – making it our own___

It's all just there – every day for us – making it our own___

Yes to being – singing it out – yes to the ease of flow___

Pure energy – bursting from eternal – love shared___

Let's take the river and ride in natural flow___

Everyone is perfectly in their journey of self and universal collaboration___

Everyone is in harmony being tuned into universal motion___

As pure as we always have been in co-creation___

As pure as we are in living ease in the now___

Remembrance Beauty Abundance___

Stillness of times glimpse our simple gift___

Awakened breath motion flow manifested___

Creations thread woven our canvas formed___

Being knowing belonging songs heart intuitive___

Beauty sun earths rhythm water life reflection___

Delight truth vision ever creating landscape___

See feel language song eternal joy as always___

Time slowed recognition ocean's breath surf's play___

Vulnerability to Courage___

Our only doing is to show up and to be loving___

Our only vulnerability the hidden long ago hurt is misunderstanding___

Release by sharing and declare – I too carry hurt come and see___

Healing by declaring sharing – this is too heavy for heart truth love___

Our only way is this open-heart clarity and renewed growth strength___

Our only action to leave behind that old way fear laced hate ego isolation___

Vulnerability to courage only through contrast dark to beauty truth___

In all those reflections varied and judged we arrive through veiled sight___

We are the greatest when we share our capacity for compassion love___

And in that giving we receive what we need in return truth eternal love___

Storm Rolling In___

And the old ego storm keeps on rolling in___

Giving contrast to see freedom when light appears anew___

Giving contrast to let ourselves unlatch from that judgement illusion fear___

And we awaken to experience talent expressed skill purpose___

Allowing group work/play in sun basking creation innovation___

In shared group vision purpose is our release from fear to love___

And the old ego storm keeps on rolling in___

The song deep humans core is always a simple cry to extend love___

To remind us in our everyday to show love is our way to soul spirit joy___

To remind us the storm shaking our hearts – is shaking us towards each other___

Conclusion___

In loving gratitude to all as we conclude this step of our work/play together___

May these simple intuitive meditative reminders find you in your eternal love___

Seeking in this human form we speak only two basic languages eternal love or fear ego___

Eternal love through thought words action is our step into evolution of the human mind___

Eternal love transforms us with freedom joy ease awareness___

All abundance is in with and throughout us in this expanding multi-verse___

Being human in eternal love is our work/play purposefully sharing our art our creation___

Our only human doing is to be in the now sharing with each other___

Sharing our eternal love to encourage all of us to awake from ego___

About the Author

Josef "Joe" Stanislaus Zubrzycki was born on May 5, 1960 in Zubrzyca Dolna, Poland and lived there with his family for the first 5 years of his life. These years formed the foundation of the intuitive understanding of wholeness within the contrasting world fragmented thoughts and beliefs apparent in current life.

Joe's educational experience took place in Chicago, Illinois beginning with grade school at St. Michael the Archangel then high school at Quigley South Preparatory Seminary. Along with a strong religious home life, these years provided a vantage point of how others interacted with their views on religion and spirituality. The next major transition in Joe's life happened at Lewis University during a course in "The Religious History of Mankind before Christ". The major text in the course was The Sacred and the Profane. The understanding was born that humans have always searched for a higher relationship with the spiritual. Thus, began Joe's truth-seeking quest about spirituality as an adult.

After just a year and a half of college Joe entered the world of restaurant business ownership with family... Zubrzycki's Warsaw Inn. He had worked in the family business as an employee since age 12. The great lessons through the next 30 years were based in the service of others, leadership and coaching. Joe achieved his greatest awareness in the contrast of abundance and scarcity depending on mindset popularly referred to as the law of attraction.

In 2010, Joe left the family business to embark on this current journey of freedom with joyful ease. This enlightenment quest started based on the release of antiquated beliefs and principles that no longer serve us. Three new businesses were started during this new chapter involving creative visionary awareness and development. A few years later inspired in part by a study of A Course in Miracles, the writing of Awake from Ego was completed with an extreme gratitude for the journey and all the wonderful encouraging souls met along the way.

About the Cover Artist

Dr. Steve Hinkey is an artist and energetic healer. As a chiropractor, Hinkey began using drawing as part of his diagnostic and therapeutic practice with patients in 1978. He often worked with patients whose cases defied traditional medical diagnosis, leading to great success with seemingly incurable conditions, severe challenges in transformation, and soon developed a large following. Steve's art bridges the Invisible and the Visible in symbol and Presence. They are a blend of abstraction, suggestion, influence, and energy that capture the essence of a Moment, and the vibrations of the environment and the people occupying his attention.

Joe attended many events called 'Healing Theater' in Chicago over several years. Dr. Steve would draw each participant to reveal their current and next step, aid the release of the past, and provide the art as a talisman to further release obstacles and integrate change.

The back cover depicts a moment of incredibly powerful breakthrough, where the purple and gold 'fire' of his central channel bursts through to his energy fields and aura, exposing him to his deeper purpose. Radiant greens depict his dominant virtue, which is being squarely upon the 'Path of Love'; while the balance of the blue throat chakra drawn as infinity is inclusionary to his desire to serve All. The strength and balance in this drawing can be seen in the way Joe produces results in all areas of his life.

The front cover is so potent a symbol of 'As above, so below' - where God and Man are reflections of each other, that Joe's healing drawing became the core symbol for Dr. Steve's art gallery installations. Depicting the fluid synthesis of all color, all Rays, in wonderful harmony, integrated and anchored in red form, walking through the ether with ease, under the watchful Eye of God… Joe's drawing teaches us how to have problems and obstacles, while at the same time having elegance and flow to stay on purpose, letting purpose itself lead us, heal us, cleanse us, modify us as needed to be ever more loving no matter what.

To see the full versions of Dr. Steve's artwork, visit www.awakefromego.com.

www.ingramcontent.com/pod-product-compliance
Lightning Source LLC
LaVergne TN
LVHW061345060426
835512LV00012B/2574